Eucharistic Adoration for Children

Jesus – please teach us to pray!

Anne Joachim

Eucharistic Adoration for Children
By Anne Joachim

This book is especially
for you, to help you
know what to do when
you visit Jesus at
church.

What is your name?

Jesus knows.

Jesus loves you.

He is looking forward
to listening to you, and
speaking to you.

How to use this book

The first part of this book is for you to read so that you understand how Jesus is specially here in Catholic churches.

The second part of this book is full of activities which will be prayerful and respectful while you are visiting Jesus.

PART ONE – READ ALL ABOUT IT!

Jesus is specially here in Catholic churches

You may already know that God created our beautiful world and that it was God's idea to make human beings!

A long time ago, you and I didn't exist. But God thought of us and created us, out of love.

Can you imagine a time before the world existed?

There was just God, and nothing and nobody else!

God loved us so much that he wanted us to be very close to him and to get to know him better.

About two thousand years ago, God sent his son, Jesus, to live with human beings on earth.

It's amazing to think that God's own son was born as a little tiny baby, and had to be looked after by his Mummy Mary, and his foster father, Joseph!

But instead of being thankful that God had sent us Jesus, some people put Jesus to death on a cross!

That didn't stop Jesus, because Jesus is God and God is all-powerful.

Jesus rose from the dead!

Forty days after Jesus rose from the dead, Jesus ascended into heaven, and we look forward to seeing him when we, too, go to heaven.

Heaven is happy because of Jesus. We are made especially to be with Jesus, and it is the only thing that makes us truly happy.

Jesus has given us a way that we can be in a sort of heaven even now, while we are still living on earth. Not everybody knows this, but it isn't a secret…

What you are about to
read is NOT…

...!

We can visit Jesus in
any Catholic church!

You will find out more
as you look through
this book.

PART TWO – ACTIVITIES TO CARRY OUT PRAYERFULLY IN CHURCH!

Look at this picture of Jesus' Last Supper. Jesus is in the middle, with a red halo around his head. The other people are his disciples.

Look at the disciples.

What do you think
they are they thinking?

How do you think they
are feeling?

What is on the table in
front of Jesus?

What do you think
Jesus is saying?

At the Last Supper, Jesus took bread and said, "This is My Body!". Then he took a cup of wine and said, "This is My Blood!".

He really meant it and the bread and wine really became his body and blood!

Every time we have
Mass, the priest says
Jesus' words again,
and the bread and
wine really become
Jesus' body and blood!

Spot the similarities and differences between these two pictures.

After Mass, Jesus is put into
a box called the tabernacle.

Can you see a
tabernacle in your
church?

What colour is it?

Look for a little light
above or beside the
tabernacle.
What colour is the
light?

When the light is lit, it
means that Jesus is in
the tabernacle.

At Adoration, Jesus is taken out of the tabernacle and is put into a monstrance so that we can all see him more easily.

Can you see a monstrance in your church?

Can you see Jesus in the middle?

This is a monstrance.

Look at Jesus lovingly
for a few minutes. He
is looking back at you
lovingly.

Pray this prayer:

Dear Jesus,

I love you. Please help
me to love you more.
Please help me to
know that you are here
with me always.
Amen.

This is another monstrance. Is it like the one in your church?

Sometimes, at Adoration, there are candles lit around the altar.

Count how many candles are lit in your church.

For each one, say quietly in your head, "Jesus, you are the light of the world."

Why do you think we
use candles in church?

Think of all the special
things you can think
about light and fire
and candles.

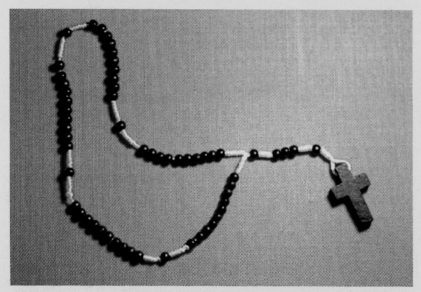

There is a lovely prayer called the Rosary. For each decade of the Rosary, you say 1 Our Father, 10 Hail Marys and 1 Glory Be. You can use your fingers or Rosary beads to count the 10 Hail Marys.

Pray the Rosary using your fingers or Rosary Beads. While you are saying the prayers in your head, think about the Institution of the Eucharist at the Last Supper, when Jesus said, "This is My Body", and look at Jesus on the altar, imagining that you are with him at the Last Supper.

Our Father, who art in heaven, hallowed be thy name. Thy kingdom come, thy will be done on earth as it is in heaven. Give us this day our daily bread and forgive us our trespasses as we forgive those who trespass against us, and lead us not into temptation but deliver us from evil, Amen.

10 times: Hail Mary, full of grace, the Lord is with thee. Blessed art thou among women and blessed is the fruit of thy womb, Jesus. Holy Mary, Mother of God, pray for us sinners now and at the hour of our death, Amen.

Glory be to the Father,
and to the Son, and to
the Holy Spirit, as it
was in the beginning is
now and ever shall be,
world without end.
Amen.

Look at Jesus on the altar.

Think about your family and friends and say,
"God bless ...."

God is good, all the time! All the time, God is good!

What other words can you think of for good (e.g. lovely, wonderful)?

Look at Jesus on the altar and tell Jesus these words, saying:

"Jesus, you are good, you are ...."

What is your favourite
animal?
Did you know, that
God made all the
animals?!

We can thank God for
all the wonderful
things he has made.

Look at Jesus on the
altar, and say THANK
YOU!
to him for all the
animals.

Can you think of an animal for every letter of the alphabet?

Start with A, and look at Jesus and say thank you to him for animals beginning with A, like ants and antelopes and anteaters and aardvarks.

Then go on to thank Jesus for animals beginning with B and keep going until you get to Z!

Do you know any hymns about thanking God?

Find a hymn book in your church and look at the index at the back for hymns beginning with 'Thank you.'

Did you know that one way of praying is to concentrate on breathing, and to imagine saying the name Jesus as you are breathing out?

Take a deep breath in, and then slowly breathe out, saying in your mind:

Repeat this ten times.

Listen…

In a moment, you will
close your eyes and listen.

What sounds can you hear
near you inside the
church?

What sounds can you hear
outside the church?

Ask God to bless all the
people responsible for the
sounds you have heard.

Remember, God made us
with two ears. Listening
must be important!

Look at Jesus on the altar
and ask him to help you to
listen to him. Then spend
a few moments quietly
listening to anything Jesus
wants to say to you.

Soon, it will be time to leave the church.

Before you go, ask Jesus to help you decide to do one thing differently from now on, so that you can show how much you love him.

Thank you for reading
this Anne Joachim
book!

We hope you loved it.

Look out for more
books by this author,
and why not take the
time to write a review?

Catholic Stories for Children — Best Friends Forever — Anne Joachim

Catholic Stories for Children — Sunday Football — Anne Joachim

Catholic Stories for Children — Christmas Carol Concert — Anne Joachim

Anne Joachim — Catholic Stories for Children — Horse Riding

Made in United States
Orlando, FL
12 June 2023

34064711R00027